Mind Your Mood

Proven Steps to Control Your Mood Swings

Dan Miller

Disclaimer

The information contained in this book is strictly for educational purpose only. The content of this book is the sole expression and opinion of its author and not necessarily that of the publisher. It is not intended to cure, treat, and diagnose any kind of disease or medical condition. It is sold with the understanding that the publisher is not rendering any type of medical, psychological, legal, or any other kind of professional advice. You should seek the services of a competent professional before applying concepts in this book. Neither the publisher nor the individual author(s) shall be liable for any physical, psychological, emotional, financial, or commercial damages, directly or indirectly by the use of this material, which is provided "as is", and without warranties. Therefore, if you wish to apply ideas contained in this book, you are taking full responsibility for your actions.

Table of Contents

Important Insight

Cognitive therapy has gained massive acceptance among mental health professionals as well as the public. As a matter of fact, cognitive therapy has become one of the most practiced and researched forms of psychotherapy in the entire universe.

There are a number of reasons that explain this growing interest. One of them stems from the fact that cognitive therapy consists of basic down-to-earth ideas that are intuitive and appealing.

Secondly, research studies have confirmed cognitive therapy to be very critical for individuals suffering from anxiety, and depression among other problems.

Thirdly, lots of self-help books have aroused a strong and popular demand for cognitive therapy not only in the United States but also the entire world.

Cognition refers to a perception or thought. In other words, cognitions describe the way you think about events or things at any particular moment. The thoughts go through your mind automatically without much control from your end. This has a huge impact on how you generally feel. For instance, people read self-help books on various subjects because of their thoughts and feelings. If they feel depressed and discouraged, they may pick an inspirational book to lift their moods.

Your feelings are a sum total of the messages you give yourself. If you think of yourself as a loser or a useless person, those thoughts will compound to form a feeling which is mapped onto your behavioral pattern. Close to 2000 years ago, Epictetus, a Greek philosopher stated that people are oftentimes disturbed not by things but rather by the views we take of them. In the Bible, the book of Proverbs 23:7 states that "For as he thinks within himself, so he is". Shakespeare in Hamlet, Act 2, and Scene 2 expresses a similar idea and says *"For there is nothing either good or bad, but thinking makes it so"*

The idea of how thinking commands your mood has been around for quite some time but many depressed people do not really understand it. When you are depressed, you may falsely think that the bad things that have happened to you are the cause of it. You may feel inferior and destined to be unhappy because someone you love rejected you or you failed in your work.

Even though no single treatment will ever be an ultimate solution, cognitive therapy has been shown by research studies to be effective in dealing with a number of disorders including depression.

This book explores the mind and how changing your moods can change your life.

1: Understanding Your Moods

Depression has been viewed throughout history as an emotional disorder and therapists including psychologists and psychiatrists have placed a strong emphasis on getting in touch with your feelings. However, recent research has revealed otherwise.

Depression is not an emotional disorder but rather the result of distorted negative thinking. A pessimistic and illogical attitude plays a central role in the continued development of depression and the accompanying symptoms.

Intense negative thinking always accompanies any painful emotion including depression. The moody thoughts you have when upset are entirely different from those you have when you are not upset. The negative thoughts that flood your mind are the driving force behind your self-defeating emotions. They keep you lethargic and burden you with the feeling of inadequacy. Unfortunately, these negative thoughts are often overlooked as the symptoms of depression even though they hold the key to relief.

Every time you feel depressed, identify a corresponding negative thought you had before the depression. Since these thoughts have contributed to your bad mood, learning to restructure them can help you change your moods. Negative thoughts are commonly referred to as automatic thoughts because they run through the mind without the slightest effort on your part. They are so natural and obvious to you just as you would hold a folk and a spoon.

The Relationship between How You Feel and the Way You Think

The first major breakthrough to understanding your moods is in knowing how your thoughts affect your feelings because your emotions result from the way you perceive things.

There is neurological evidence that before experiencing any event, your mind first processes it and then gives it a meaning. You must understand what is happening to you and around you before you can feel it. Where the understanding is accurate, your emotions will then be normal. However, if your perception is twisted in some way, your emotional response will also be abnormal.

Depression falls in the category of twisted perception. The cause of your blue moods can be linked to scratchy music that comes from a radio that is not tuned properly to the station. The problem is not the transmitters, the tubes or the signal coming from the radio station.

The only thing you need is to adjust your dials and the station becomes clear. As a human being, you must learn how to bring about mental tuning so that your music will also come through clearly and your depression will lift.

When you are depressed, you possess a remarkable ability to marshal people around you to believe that what you are going through is indeed a reality while it is just an illusion. The work of therapists is to penetrate that veil of illusion and to look behind the mirrors so that you can see how you have been bullying and fooling yourself.

Cognitive Distortions

Below is a list of cognitive distortions that form the foundation and basis of all your depressions. Whenever you feel upset, this list will help you to decolonize your thoughts and reason in a much more sober way.

All or Nothing Thinking

This is a tendency to evaluate your qualities in extreme; either black or white. For instance, someone may tell you - If I lose this one, I am nothing. An "A" student who receives a "B" in an exam can easily conclude that he is a total failure.

All or nothing thinking is the basis for perfectionism. It makes you fear any mistake because a slight loss is magnified to mean a total disaster. People with this thinking feel worthless and inadequate.

When you evaluate things in this manner, you become unrealistic because life is never completely one way or the other. It is a mixture of ups and downs and lefts and rights. For instance, there is no one who is totally stupid or absolutely brilliant. Also, no one is totally ugly or completely attractive. If you would take time to look at the floor in the room you are seated, you will notice that is not perfectly clean.

Absolutes do not exist in this world. The moment you force your experiences into absolute categories, you will constantly suffer depression because your perceptions will not be in tandem with reality. As a matter of fact, you will be setting yourself up for endless discrediting because whatever you do will never measure up to the exaggerated expectations that you have. This ultimately creates a perceptual error known as dichotomous thinking.

Overgeneralization

Every time you over-generalize, you are in essence concluding arbitrarily that something that happened to you once will resurface over and over again and if what happened is unpleasant, the mere thought of it makes you feel upset. One depressed salesman saw a bird dung on his car window and he thought within himself that was his luck. When asked about this experience, he quickly admitted that in his twenty years of travelling, he could not remember a time when he found bird dung on his vehicle window.

The pain of rejection is another aspect that is generated from overgeneralization. Where the pain of rejection is absent, a personal affront may be a bit disappointing but not seriously disturbing. One young man gathered up his courage and asked a girl for a date. When the lady politely declined because of a previous commitment, the man started saying to himself that he is never going to get a girl to date because no girl will accept him.

In his distorted cognitions, he made a quick conclusion that because he was turned down once, it will happen over and over again. He also entertained thoughts that since all women have identical tastes, he would be repeatedly rejected by every eligible woman.

Mental Filter

This happens when you pick out a single negative detail in any particular situation and dwell on it exclusively hence seeing the whole situation as negative. For instance, a college student who was depressed had his fellow students ridiculing her best friend.

She instantly became furious because she thought the human race has become insensitive and cruel. What she was overlooking was the fact that in the previous months nobody has been cruel to her and this was just an isolated event happening to her friend.

In another occasion after she had taken her exams, she was pretty sure that she had gotten approximately 17 questions out of 100 wrong. She dwelt exclusively on these 17 questions and even thought how she would escape out of college because of the imminent embarrassment. When the results came up, the tutor was so much pleased with her because her grade was by far the highest.

Depression gives you a pair of eye glasses which filter out anything positive and allows your mind to enter into a negative pit. Because the filtering process happens rather unconsciously, you begin concluding that everything is negative. This process of filtering out the positive and admitting the negative is known as selective abstraction and is a bad habit which can potentially cause you to suffer needless anguish.

Disqualifying the Positive

This is a spectacular mental illusion present in depressed individuals which gives them a tendency to transform both neutral and positive experiences into negative ones. They ignore positive experiences and cleverly turn into negative ones a process known as reverse alchemy.

If you are depressed, you may develop a strange tendency for doing the exact opposites. For instance, you can instantly transform joy into emotional lead. The interesting thing is that all these conversions happen unconsciously.

A day-to-day example of disqualifying the positive is the manner in which we have been conditioned to respond to compliments. When a colleague or a family member compliments you, you may start thinking they are just being nice. This is how you mentally disqualify a compliment with one swift blow. If you constantly throw cold water on good things that happen to you, life will always seem chilly and damp.

Disqualifying the positive is arguably one of the most destructive types of cognitive distortion. By discrediting the positives, you are behaving like a scientist looking for evidence to support some hypothesis. In your case, the hypothesis dominating your depressive kind of thinking is that of being second rate.

This form of cognitive distortion has the potential to cause some of the most intractable and extreme forms of depression. For instance, one person who was hospitalized for severe depression said no one could care for him because he is such an awful person.

Once she was discharged, staff members and other patients expressed great fondness for her. In response she said, all those people never count because they do not see him in his real world. He never believed that a real person outside the hospital would ever care about him.

By disqualifying positive experiences in this way, he can maintain a constant negative belief which is inconsistent and unrealistic with his day-to-day experiences. Negative thinking and inadvertent ignorance of positive things removes the richness of life and makes things appear bleak.

Jumping into Conclusions

At times, people arbitrarily jump into negative conclusions without examining the facts on the table. This is best illustrated in the fortune teller error and mind reading.

In mind reading, the victims make assumptions that others are looking down on them and they are so convinced that they do not want to look out for evidence to the contrary.

For instance, if you are delivering a speech and someone in the front row starts nodding off because of exhaustion and hangovers from the previous night, you may think the audience is bored with your speech.

If a friend passes you by on the street without saying hello because he hasn't even noticed you, you may erroneously conclude that he is ignoring you or does not like you anymore.

Without much thinking and putting things into perspective, you may start reacting by either counter attack or withdrawal. This is a self-defeating behavior which ultimately acts as a self-fulfilling prophesy. Through your reaction, people will indeed avoid you and you will be a loner.

The fortune teller error on the other hand is based on false imagination that something bad is going to happen and you take this as an absolute fact despite it being unrealistic. One student repeatedly told herself that she was going to pass out or go crazy because of anxiety attacks.

These predictions were not true because she had never passed out let along gone crazy in her whole life. However, this negative prediction caused her to feel hopeless.

Jumping into conclusions is something we do on a regular basis. If you call a friend and they fail to return your call within the reasonable time, you may think that they have ignored you or they were not much interested to call you back. This may ultimately lead you to avoid them.

Magnification and Minimization

This is a thinking trap that many people fall into. Specialists call it a binocular trick because you are either shrinking things or blowing them out of proportion. Magnification occurs when you look at your fears, errors or imperfections and exaggerate them.

You turn common negative events into nightmarish monsters. Looking at your strength, you may do the exact opposite. Instead of magnifying your talents and abilities, you are minimizing them and this makes you feel inferior and useless.

Emotional Reasoning

This is when you take your emotions to act as evidence for the truth. Emotional reasoning is misleading because your feelings reflect the nature of your beliefs and thoughts. Where the thoughts are distorted, your emotions will have no validity.

For instance, someone may say that they feel guilty; therefore they must have done something bad. Emotional reasoning plays an active role in almost all depression cases. Because things feel negative to you, you immediately assume that they truly must be.

In addition to these forms of cognitive distortions is the aspect of should statements. The moment you begin directing should statements toward other people, you will in the end feel frustrated. "Should statements" generate unnecessary emotional turmoil in your life.

Whenever the reality of your own behavior doesn't match your standard, your "should" and "shouldn't" often create guilt, shame and self-loathing. You have to change your perception in order to approximate reality or you will always feel let down by others.

2: Building Your Self-Esteem

Depression makes you believe that you are worthless; the severe the depression, the greater the feeling of worthlessness. According to a survey conducted, over 80 percent of patients suffering depression express self-dislike. The findings also reveal that depressed patients perceive themselves as being deficient in achievement, intelligence, attractiveness, popularity, strength and health. A depressed self-image is often characterized by defeat, defect, desertedness and deprivation.

Almost every negative emotional emotion inflicts damage because of low self-esteem. A poor self-image is more or less like a magnifying glass which can transform a trivial imperfection or mistake into an overwhelming symbol of defeat. The affected people seem convinced that when one person looks down upon them then the whole world will reject them. It is as if the rejection was rubber stumped on their forehead for everyone to see. Their sense of self-esteem is low and they measure themselves by how others look at them.

The most tragic thing is that depressed people do not see their problems as being unrealistic and self-defeating. Instead, they feel convinced that they are worthless and inferior making any suggestion to the contrary sound foolish and dishonest. When you are depressed, you become persistent and so persuasive that you lead family, friends and other people around you to accept your maladaptive belief that you are defective and useless.

The manner in which a therapist handles your feelings of inadequacy is very important as far as the cure is concerned. The critical question to ask is - What is the genuine source of self-esteem? One of the realities that you have to accept is you cannot earn worth through what you do.

Achievements may bring satisfaction but certainly not happiness. Self-worth that is based on accomplishments is not genuine but pseudo esteem. Many people are successful but still depressed. In a similar manner, you cannot base your self-worthiness on your talent, fortune, fame and looks.

A lot of people who go through depression are in fact loved by friends and family but this doesn't help because self-esteem and self-worth are missing. The bottom line to all this is that your own self-worth is the determinant to how you feel.

The first step into gaining your self-worth is closely looking at what you are telling yourself. The evidence that you put forward to defend your worthlessness is usually nonsensical. A recent scientific study conducted by Dr. David Braff and Aaron Beck indicated that depressed patients undergo a formal thinking disturbance. Just like schizophrenic patients, depressed persons make logical errors in extracting meaning from sayings and proverbs. They cannot make accurate generalization.

According to the study, depression patients lose some of their capacity to think clearly and have trouble putting things in their proper perspective. Negative events become so important to them and they dominate their entire reality making it difficult for them to tell that their thoughts are distorted. They create the illusion of hell and make it very convincing. The more depressed and miserable they feel, the more twisted their thinking becomes.

The most common mental distortion that comes to us when depressed is the all-or-nothing thinking. This perception makes you see life in extreme categories where you believe that your performance is terrible or great - nothing in between. This type of self evaluation is unrealistic and creates an overwhelming disappointment and anxiety.

Overcoming the Feeling of Worthlessness

Dealing with your self-esteem is a crucial step towards improving your mood and self-image. There are several techniques that are specific and easy to apply that can help you develop a sense of worth. If you keep on practicing and working on them, you will experience one of the fastest and most enduring personal growths.

Talking back to the Internal Critic

The sense of worthlessness is often created by your internal dialogue. Through statements that degrade you such as I am inferior, I am not any good, and I am a failure, you are creating a feeling of despair and poor self-esteem. In order to overcome this, you should take the following steps:

- Train yourself to write down all the self-critical thoughts as they go through your mind

- Understand why these thoughts are distorted

- Practice talking back to them and develop a realistic self-evaluation system

The Triple Column Technique

Using the triple column technique, you can accomplish this. Divide a piece of paper into three columns and label the left hand column self-criticism, the middle column as cognitive distortion, and the right hand column as self-defense. In the left hand column, put down every hurtful self-criticism you make when you are feeling worthless.

For instance, if you realize you are late for a meeting, your heart sinks and you are gripped with panic. At that moment, jot down the thoughts that are going through your mind. Because these are the very thoughts that cause your emotional upset that rip away at you, you should carefully note them.

The second step is to list the cognitive distortions that we discussed in the previous chapter. Go through them and see whether you can identify the thinking errors in each of your automatic thoughts.

For instance, if you say to yourself that you never do anything right in the left column, this is an example of a thought that fits in the overgeneralization category of cognitive distortions. This step prepares you for mood transformation where you substitute the destructive thoughts with more rational and less upsetting ones in the right hand column.

Do not cheer yourself up by saying things that you do not believe are valid. Instead, you should recognize the truth. Make sure you completely believe in your rebuttal to self-criticism. This rational response in the right hand column will take into account what was illogical and erroneous about your automatic thought.

If you cannot think of a rational response to a particular negative thought, forget about it for a while. Maybe a few days later, it will come back to you. This way, you will give yourself an opportunity to see the other side of the coin. Work on the triple column technique for about 15 minutes every day for a period of about one or two months. With time, it will become much easier.

Do not fear asking friends and colleagues how they would answer a certain upsetting thought if you cannot figure out the appropriate response on your own.

One thing that you need to carefully note is that in the automatic thought column, you should not describe your emotional reaction rather write the thoughts that caused the emotion. For example, if you notice a flat tire on your car, do not write I feel crappy. Instead, write down the thoughts that automatically came into your mind when you saw the flat tire. One of the thought could be – I am so stupid I should have carried a spare tire. On the right hand column, you then write something like – I am not stupid because I just happened to forget the tire at home. This process of rationalizing your negative thoughts will not inflate your tires but it will prevent a deflated ego.

In as much as describing your emotions is not appropriate in the automatic thought column, it is helpful to do emotional accounting before and after the triple column technique. This will help you determine the extent to which your feelings have improved.

Daily Record of Dysfunctional Thoughts

Apart from the triple column technique, there is the daily record of dysfunctional thoughts. This allows you to record your upsetting thoughts, feelings and the trigger behind the negative event. Suppose you are selling insurance policies and a customer happens to insult you without any reason and goes ahead to hang up on you.

On the daily record of dysfunctional thoughts, jot down the actual event in the situation column. Thereafter, write down your feelings and the distorted thoughts that created them in the correct column. Finally, talk back to each of these thoughts and do an emotional accounting. The beauty with the daily record of dysfunctional thoughts is that it allows you to analyze your negative thoughts, events and feelings in an extremely systematic way.

The choice of the technique to use is totally up to you. By simply taking the challenge of answering your negative thoughts with responses that are rational on a day-to-day basis, you will ultimately change your thinking. Writing them down is important because it forces you to develop much more objectivity than you could ever achieve where your responses swirl in your mind. Writing down also helps you to locate the mental errors that are responsible for your depression.

The triple column technique not only deals with personal inadequacy problems but also handles other emotional difficulties caused by distorted thinking.

Mental Biofeedback

This method is useful in monitoring your negative thoughts using a wrist counter. A wrist counter is much more like a wrist watch and you can buy one from a sporty goods store or a golf shop. It has a push button which changes the number on the dial every time it is pressed. When a negative thought goes through your mind, press the push button. By the end of the day, go through your daily total score and note it down.

At the beginning, you will realize your number increasing but after several days as you getter better in identifying your critical thoughts, you will see the daily total reaching a plateau before coming down. This shows your harmful thoughts diminishing and you are getting better by day.

In order to build your self-esteem you must learn how to cope and not absorb failures into your thought pattern. Do not view yourself as worthless because this type of criticism will incapacitate you and create an impression that your problem is so big that no one can do anything about it. Remove your destructive labels and find your true identity.

3: Lack of Motivation and Inactivity

Human beings are much more than thinkers; they are also doers. As a second major approach to mood elevation, you can substantially change the way you feel through your actions. The only problem with this approach is that when you are depressed, you often do not feel like doing anything.

A common destructive aspect of depression is the manner in which it paralyses your willpower. You will find yourself procrastinating even the simplest chores. With time, your lack of motivation intensifies and every activity that you undertake appears difficult and overwhelming.

This will lead you into accomplishing very little and as a result you will feel worse by day. You will cut yourself from the normal sources of stimulation and pleasure, and your productivity will take a nosedive further aggravating your self-hatred.

As long as you don't recognize that you are in an emotional prison, the situation may continue for weeks, months or even years. If you once took pride in the energy you had for life, your lack of activity will even be more frustrating. It will affect your friends, family and all those people around you who cannot understand your change in behavior. Some of them may even criticize you with hurtful comments which only worsen your paralysis and anguish.

Inactivity is one of the paradoxes of human nature. Some people find it so natural to jump into life with great energy and zest while others barely hang back with self-defeating thoughts at every turn. If a person was condemned to spend months away in isolation and cut off from all the activities and interpersonal relationship, depression would result.

Research shows that even young monkeys enter into a withdrawn and retarded state if they are confined in a cage and separated from their peers.

By doing nothing and allowing depression to isolate you, you are in essence putting yourself in a small cage and voluntarily imposing a similar punishment to that of the monkey. Cognitive techniques help you in discovering the precise reasons why it is so difficult to motivate yourself.

Through experience, therapists have seen depression patients improving substantially in instances when they try to help themselves. At times, it does not really matter what you do as long as you do it with the attitude of self-help.

Misconceptions of Procrastination and Self Defeating Behavior

Procrastination and self-defeating behavior may look frustrating, funny, infuriating, puzzling or pathetic depending on the angle that you look at it. On the contrary, this is a normal human trait which is so widespread that at one point or the other, we bump into it. Philosophers, writers and students have tried formulating explanations for self-defeating behavior throughout history. Each of the explanations represented a different psychological theory and unfortunately each of them was inaccurate.

The first trait model viewed inactivity as a fixed personality trait that stemmed from your lazy streak. The problem with this model is that it labels the problem without giving a sufficient explanation. Labeling yourself as lazy is self-defeating and useless because it creates a pseudo impression that your lack of motivation is an innate and irreversible part of your genetic makeup. This kind of thinking is not valid but rather an example of cognitive distortion.

The second model implied that all you want is to hurt yourself and suffer more because there is something desirable and enjoyable about procrastination. This theory is widespread and enormously supported by both patients and psychotherapists.

If you like doing nothing or being depressed then you need to remind yourself that depression is one of the worst form of human suffering. There is no one who enjoys the misery of depression and the suffering that comes from pain.

The third hypothesis formulated is that you are passive-aggressive and all you want is to frustrate the people around you. One of the problems with this theory is that depressed or procrastinating individuals do not feel particularly angry. Resentment can sometimes contribute to lack of motivation and is mostly not central to the problem.

Even if your family feels frustrated about your depression, it is not your intention to make them react that way. The implication that you are intentionally doing something to frustrate them is untrue and insulting and any such suggestion will make you feel worse.

The last theory suggests that getting depressed gives you some payoff. This theory holds that your moods and actions are the result of rewards and punishment from the environment. If you feel depressed and do nothing to eliminate the depression, it then follows that your behavior is being rewarded in some way.

There is an element of truth in this theory because depressed people sometimes receive support and reassurance from others who volunteer to help them.

However, the truth is that the depressed person does not enjoy the attention he receives because inside him is a tendency to disqualify the attention. Take an instance where you are depressed and someone tells you that they like you. The first thought that will cross your mind is that the other person does not know how rotten you are. If he knew, he could not have given you the praise.

Finding the Real Cause of Motivation Paralysis

The study of mood disorders places us at a vantage point where we observe extraordinary transformation in personal motivation within specific periods of time. It is true that the person who ordinarily bursts with creative energy and enviable optimism may be reduced to pathetic and bedridden mobility during episodes of depression.

Tracing dramatic mood swings enables you to gather valuable clues that help in unlocking the mysteries of human motivation. Take a step and ask yourself – What comes into mind when I think about an undone task. Write down all those thoughts on a piece of paper.

What you have just written reflects a number of maladaptive misconceptions, attitudes and faulty assumptions. One thing you learn is that the feelings that often impede your motivation such as anxiety, apathy, and the sense of being overwhelmed are simply products of distorted thinking.

The thoughts that go inside the mind of a depression patient are often negative. He thinks of how he is a loser and bound to fail hence he doesn't find the motivation of doing anything. Such thoughts may be very convincing when you are in the pit of depression but they immobilize you, overwhelm you leaving you feeling inadequate and helpless.

The tragedy comes when you take your negative thoughts and use them to justify your pessimistic attitudes. This changes your approach to life because you are totally convinced that anything you do will fail hence there is no need of even trying. You somehow lie on your bed, stare at the ceiling and hope that you will drift to sleep. Some people even refuse to answer their telephone because they fear hearing bad news.

The relationship between your feelings, thoughts and behaviors is reciprocal. Every action and emotion is a product of your thoughts and attitudes.

In a similar manner, your feelings and behavioral patterns influence your perception in a number of ways.

All emotional change is ultimately caused by cognitions. Changing your behavior will make you a little bit better if it exerts a positive influence on your thinking. It is possible to modify your self-defeating mindset if you manage to change your behavior in such a manner as to simultaneously counter the self-defeating lie that represents the core of your motivation problem.

Mindsets Associated with Procrastination and Inactivity

There are certain mindsets that are associated with your lack of activity and motivation. Going through them carefully may help you identify with either one or more of them.

Hopelessness

When you are depressed, you get stuck in the pain of the present moment that you forget you had good times in the past and wish away any possibility of future bliss. At this moment, any activity will seem useless because you are very sure your lack of motivation is irreversible and unending.

Helplessness

When you are convinced that your moods are caused by factors out of your control such as hormone cycles, fate, and genetic factors, you may find it difficult to do anything that makes you feel better.

Overwhelming Self

There are a number of ways you can overwhelm yourself to a point that you do nothing. You may at times magnify a task to such a degree that it seems impossible to handle. The mere thought that you must do everything at a go instead of breaking down each job into small manageable units to be completed one step at a time can overwhelm you. You may also distract yourself from a particular task by becoming overly obsessed with endless other things that you have not completed yet.

To give you a feel of how ridiculous this is, assume when you sit down for a meal you imagine about the food that you will eat during your entire lifetime. The vegetables, the meats, the ice creams, and thousands of fluids can overwhelm you. In the same manner, if you think about everything else at the moment, you may feel ineffective and as such expect little or nothing at all from yourself.

Undervaluing the Rewards

When you are going through depression, you may fail to do anything not because you find the task difficult but because you feel the reward is not worth the effort. The technical name given to admonished ability to experience pleasure and satisfaction is anhedonia. If you constantly discredit your efforts, you will eventually torpedo your sense of fulfillment.

Perfectionism

Inappropriate standards and goals can set you up for defeat. If you imagine settling for anything less than a magnificent performance, you will become dissatisfied and hence do nothing.

Fear of Failure

This is a mindset which can paralyze you into doing nothing. When you think about the effort you put in and yet not succeed, you become overwhelmed and refuse to try anything at all. The fear of failure is fueled by the overgeneralization thinking era. There is a tendency to reason that if you fail in one thing, you will fail in everything. Another mindset which contributes to the fear of failure is thinking about the product rather than the process. You need to understand that you can only control the process but never the outcome.

Fear of Criticism or Disapproval

When you imagine that trying something new will lead you into making a mistake that others will disprove and criticize you for, you may freeze into doing nothing. At times the risk of rejection is so dangerous that you feel the best way to protect yourself is to adopt a low profile.

Low Frustration Tolerance

It is human to assume that you could solve all your problems and reach your goals very fast and easily. This makes you go into a state of panic when obstacles come your way.

Instead of persisting and remaining patient, you retaliate and fold up everything. This is often called the entitlement syndrome because you strongly feel and act as if you are entitled to success, perfect health, love and happiness.

Countering Inactivity

To counter the above causes of inactivity and procrastination, you need to organize your tasks into a daily activity schedule with an hour-by-hour plan of the things you want to accomplish each day.

At the end of the day, fill out a retrospective column of the things that you managed to do. The daily activity schedule can help you overcome the weekend/holiday blues which is a pattern of depression common among people who are single and have enormous emotional difficulties when alone. You can also try the anti-procrastination sheet which is a form that helps you to break the habit of procrastination.

In addition to the tools above, bringing along your daily record of dysfunctional thoughts can also help you when you feel overwhelmed and pressed hard by the urge to do nothing.

4: How to Counter External Criticism

The cause of your self-worthlessness is oftentimes your ongoing self criticism. This may take the form of an upsetting internal conversation in which you persecute and harangue yourself in an unrealistic and harsh manner. Most of the times, your inner criticism has its trigger in an external remark made by someone else. Criticism whether good or bad can be an important learning point in your life. However, if you don't have the necessary techniques for handling it, criticism can be extremely dreadful.

Criticism seems so hurtful to some people while others remain undisturbed even in the face of fiercest attacks. This chapter concentrates on some of the secrets that make people face disapproval fearlessly and the steps to take in order to overcome your vulnerability to criticism. Overcoming your fear of criticism requires practice but at the same time it is not develop and master.

Before delving deeper into the techniques for overcoming criticism, you must understand that it is not the critical comments that people make that upset you irrespective of how vicious, heartless and cruel they are. They have no power to cause discomfort or disturb you even a little bit.

When a person criticizes you, there are certain negative thoughts that are triggered in your kind. These thought then create your emotional reactions and not what the other person says. The same mental errors discussed earlier will be contained in these thoughts that ultimately upset you.

Steps to Overcoming Fear of Criticism

The first step in dealing with your fear of criticism rests right in your mental processes. You should learn how to identify negative thoughts when you are criticized. You can write these thoughts down and slowly analyze them in order to see where your thinking is wrong or illogical. Thereafter, write down the rational responses which are normally less upsetting and more reasonable.

When people criticize you, the comments they make will either be right or wrong. If those comments are wrong, then you have no reason to be upset. On the other hand, if the criticism is right, there is no reason to feel overwhelmed. Just acknowledge the error and proceed to correct it.

At times, we fear criticism because we feel we need the support and approval of other people in order for us to be happy. This will lead you into devoting all your energies to pleasing people and you will have nothing much left for your own creativity and productive living.

Respond with Empathy

When someone is attacking or criticizing you, their motive may be to help you or to hurt you. To achieve this, they may say something that is right, wrong or somewhere in between. Instead of focusing on what they are saying, ask them specific questions that are designed to find out exactly what they mean. Avoid being judgmental or defensive as you probe your critic.

By asking these questions, you are in essence minimizing the possibility that the other person will reject you completely. This technique is effective in diffusing any hostility and anger and instead introduces a problem solving orientation instead of debate and blame casting.

Disarming the Critic

When someone starts attacking you, you have three choices at your disposal. The first choice is to resist and shoot back. However, this leads to mutual destruction and warfare. The second choice is to dodge the bullets or run away, but this can cause humiliation and low-esteem. The third and final choice is to stay calm and skillfully disarm your opponent. This is by far the best solution. When you take the wind out of your critic's sails, you will end up a winner and your opponent will also feel the same.

To achieve this, you have to find some way of agreeing with your opponent whether they are right or wrong. The agreement can either be in principle with the criticism or you can find some truth in the statement and agree with it. Always find some way of agreeing with what they say, avoid sarcasm or self-defense and always speak the truth. This will make the critic lose steam and before long, he will run out of bullets because instead of fighting back you are agreeing with them. As the critic cools down, he will be in a sober mood where you can communicate.

Feedback and Negotiation

After you have listened to your critic using empathy and disarmed him through agreement, you can then explain your emotions and position tactfully and negotiate any differences. If the critic is wrong, you can still express your point in a non-destructive manner by making it clear that you stand to be corrected. Ensure the conflict is based on fact and not pride or personality. Do not direct destructive labels at your critic because by simply being erroneous, it doesn't mean that he is inferior, worthless or stupid.

As you negotiate with your critic, you have a number of options that you can pursue. For instance, if he keeps on undermining you, you have the space to make your point again and again but in a more assertive and polite manner. Remember the most important thing is how you express your feelings.

Anti-heckler Technique

This is particularly useful for people who are into lecturing, teaching or delivering public speeches. You will notice that the hecklers comments have some characteristics in common. They are overly critical but grossly inaccurate, they come from a person who is not well regarded or accepted among his peers, and they are often expressed in an abusive style.

Through the Anti-heckler technique, you can effectively get away from the criticism unharmed. First of all, thank the person for their comments, acknowledge they are important and emphasize the need for more knowledge concerning the area on which the points have been raised.

You can even encourage the heckler to do further research and investigation on the particular issues. When you pursue this technique, most often than not, the heckler will come to you after the session to appreciate you for your kind comments.

In summary, how you deal with external criticism is all in your mind. If you change the way you think about your critics, you will definitely feel much more in control even when the fiercest of the salvos are fired against you.

5: Understanding Your Irritability Quotient

Your irritability quotient (IQ) refers to the level of annoyance or anger that you tend to absorb in your daily life. Where your IQ is high, you become disadvantaged because you overreact to disappointments and frustrations by creating feelings of resentment which blacken your disposition and make your life difficult. Using a rating scale of 0 to 4, you can estimate the level of your IQ.

0 – Feeling very little or no annoyance

1 – Feeling a little irritated

2 – Feeling moderately upset

3 – Feeling quite angry

4 – Feeling very angry

Using the scale above, you can pick any situation you go through and rate it. For instance, you can pick an instance where you are driving to the airport to pick a friend and you are forced to wait for an extremely long freight train. Depending on how irritating or upsetting the situation, you can assign it a value.

After you finish taking your anger inventory, you can now calculate your IQ. Add up the score for each incident you have listed. If you had 25 incidents then your maximum points should be 100 while your minimum should be 0.

You can now interpret the scores based on the below guideline:

- 0 to 45 – Within this range, the amount of annoyance and anger that you experienced is appreciably low. Only a few people manage a score within this range.

- 46 to 55 – Within this gap, you are more peaceful than the average population.

- 56 to 75 – Your response to the annoyances of life is with average amount of anger

- 86 to 100 – This is a boiling zone where you are plagued by constant and intense furious reactions that do not disappear as quickly. There is a possibility that you harbor negative feelings even after the cause of annoyance is long gone. Most people in this category are hotheads or fire crackers and experience frequent tensions, headaches as well as elevated blood pressure.

Ways of Managing Anger

Having known about your irritability quotient, you should now devise ways of handling it. Traditionally, the public including the psychotherapists have conceptualized two primary ways of dealing with anger and this is anger turned outward or anger turned inward. When you turn anger inward, you internalize your aggression and absorb your resentment like a sponge. Ultimately, this corrodes you and leads to depression and guilt.

The second approach where you turn your anger outward is where you ventilate your feelings. Although this seems to be the better of the two, it is a bit simplistic and experience shows that it does not work very well. Where you ventilate your anger everywhere you go, people will soon see you as a loony.

The third option transcends both of these approaches. This is where you stop creating your anger. This cognitive solution does not have the option of either holding or letting out your anger because it does not exist in the first place.

Identify the Source of Your Anger

It is natural for you to believe that certain external events are the source of your frustration or upset. When you become mad at someone, there is a tendency of making them the cause of all your bad feelings.

This line of thought leads you to fooling yourself because people cannot make you angry rather it is all in your mind. It does not matter how outrageous or unfair how other people may appear to you, they will never upset you. As a matter of fact, it is you who is creating every last bit of the outrage.

Just like all other emotions, anger is created by your thoughts. You will note that before feeling irritated by events, you must first become aware of what is happening and interpret it in your own way. Your feelings will result from the meaning you give to a particular event rather than the event itself.

There are external events which are caused by people and certainly out of control. Internal events on the other hand are totally within your control. Your emotional reaction is determined entirely by what you think about the situation.

In many instances, your anger is created by cognitive distortions. Just like depression, many of your perceptions are one sided, twisted and plainly wrong. Once you learn how to replace the distorted thoughts with more functional and realistic ones, you will feel less irritated and you will gain greater self-control.

Among the cognitive distortions that creep into your mind through moments of anger are labeling where you describe the other person with all sorts of names because you see him in a totally negative light. When you label someone, you are in fact creating the impression that they have a bad essence. Mental filtering is the other distortion that comes during these moments where because of a single incident; you disqualify all the positives that the person has.

Only one person in the entire world has the power to threaten your self-esteem and that is simply you. If you put yourself down, your sense of self-worth will also go down. The most real and practical solution is to put to an end your inner harangue.

Develop the Desire

Anger is one of the most difficult emotions to modify because when you get mad, persuading you to stop is extremely tough. The desire for revenge consumes you and it becomes almost impossible to get rid of the hurtful feelings.

Anger is caused by your perception about what is unfair and as such you will be extremely hesitant to let go of the feeling. To get rid of this, you may consider listing the advantages and disadvantages of your anger and the contemplated retaliation. You have to look at both the short term and long term impacts of your anger. After that, review and ask yourself which pros and cons are greater. This will open your eyes and determine whether your resentment truly serves you.

Cool Your Hot Thoughts

When you have decided to cool down, one of the ways you can use is to write down all the hot thoughts that are going through your mind. Then you can gradually replace them with more objective and less upsetting cool thoughts.

Imagining Technique

The negative thoughts going through your mind in moments of anger can be linked to the script of an X-rated movie that you project into your mind. The daydreams images and fantasies of violence and revenge can be pleasant and colorful. Unless you deliberately look for these images, you may not see them. Nevertheless, they affect you strongly and their influence can be negatively or positively arousing just as any erotic dreams or nightmares.

The images keep your anger alive for long even after the initial insult has occurred. You are the one creating the anger because you have chosen to put up the images in your mind for long instead of discarding them. You are simply the director and producer of your own film and worse, you are the only one in the audience.

To take control of your irritability quotient, you must rewrite the rules. Any unrealistic rules about personal relationship may end up making you upset and frustrated. You can begin rewriting your script today by changing your expectation and giving up your anger. This will change your feelings for the better and give you a much more peaceful coexistence.

6: Ways of Handling Guilt

Psychologists, philosophers, writers and spiritual leaders have grappled with the question concerning the origin of guilt. Some have put forward that guilt comes from sin, others postulate that guilt is a helpful and realistic component of human existence, while others dismiss it as a useless emotion that human beings would be better without.

Guilt is an emotion you experience when you think about something you have done which you shouldn't have or vice versa. Also, when you point towards a certain bad behavior that you have which labels you as a bad person, you will be walking around with a guilt neck tag. The concept of labeling yourself as being bad is the center of guilt. Without the feelings of badness, even the most hurtful actions may lead to a healthy feeling of remorse but not guilt.

Remorse refers to the undistorted awareness that you unnecessarily and willfully acted in a manner that was hurtful towards yourself or others. Remorse is different from guilt because there is no implication your hurtful behavior indicates that you are inherently bad, immoral or evil.

In a nut shell, remorse is aimed at a particular behavior while guilt is targeted toward oneself. If you feel shame, depression or anxiety in addition to your guilt, it is probably due to the following assumptions:

- Feeling of worthlessness or inferiority because of your bad behavior – This leads top depression
- Feeling that others will look down on you if they found out what you did – This leads to shame
- Feeling of being in danger of punishment or retaliation – This provokes anxiety

The best and simplest way of assessing whether the feelings created by your thoughts are destructive or useful, you need to determine if they have any of the cognitive distortions described earlier. Where these thinking errors are present, your depression, anxiety and guilt cannot be realistic or valid.

The Guilt Cycle

Once you begin feeling guilty, your thoughts and feelings get entrapped in an illusion which constantly justifies that your guilt is valid. Such illusions are often convincing and powerful. Your guilt will convince you that you are indeed bad and take you to another level of guilt.

This cognitive-emotional connection ultimately locks your feelings and thoughts into each other. In the long run, you will find yourself in a circular system known as the guilt cycle.

This cycle is fueled by emotional reasoning. There is an automatic assumption that simply because you are feeling guilty, there must be a possibility that you have fallen short in one or the other way and you deserve to suffer. This is irrigational because by self loathing, you do not necessarily prove that what you did was wrong.

Your guilt is a mere reflection of the fact that you believe you behaved badly. For instance, children may be frequently punished often inappropriately because the parents are irritable, tired or misinterpret their behaviors. In these situations, the guilt of the child does not prove that he did anything wrong.

Through self-punishing behavior, your guilt cycle intensifies. Ultimately, your guilt provoking thoughts will make you unproductive and further reinforce your belief that you are bad.

The Irresponsibility of Guilt

Ask yourself these questions – If you do something wrong or hurtful, do you deserve to suffer? If yes, for how long must you suffer? What nature of sentence will you impose on yourself? At the expiry of your self-imposed sentence, are you willing to stop suffering and making yourself miserable?

If your answer is to the affirmative, then it would at least be a responsible way to punish yourself because of the time limit. However, there is no need in the first place of abusing yourself with guilt.

Your sense of guilt will in no way reverse your mistakes or speed your learning process so as to avoid the same mistakes in the future. People will not love and respect you more because of putting yourself down under the weight of sin.

The question then comes – How do you behave morally and control your impulses if you do not feel guilt? The way you view yourself after a hurtful impact on others will determine your level of guilt.

You have to recognize that you have made a mistake and develop a corrective strategy to deal with the problem. You need to wear an attitude of relaxation and self-love to facilitate this correction.

You can replace your sense of guilt with a basis for moral behavior such as empathy. Empathy gives you the ability to visualize the either good or bad consequence of your behavior. It gives you the capacity to conceptualize the effect of what you do on others and even yourself so you can feel genuine and appropriate sorrow without necessarily labeling yourself as bad.

Daily Record of Dysfunctional Thoughts

Through the daily record of dysfunctional thoughts that was introduced in the earlier chapters, you can get rid of unwanted emotions including guilt. Record the event that activates your guilt in the column labeled situation. Then identify the cognitive distortions and write down more sober and objective thoughts. This will give you relief.

Rid Yourself of Should Statements

You also need to remove the "should statements" which are often irrational. You can achieve this by rewriting the rules that govern your behavior and making them more valid. By substituting other words for should such as "it would be nice if" or "I wish I could", you can successfully sound less upsetting and more realistic.

Stick to Your Guns

One of the biggest disadvantages of guilt is that others may use the opportunity to manipulate you. If you feel obligated to please everybody including your friends and family, they may use this opportunity to push you into doing lots of things that may not necessarily be to your best interest.

By sticking to your guns, you may attract criticism from others who may believe you are wounding them by not accepting their requests. However, this should not bother you because in the long run, this principle will save you from hurtful and guilt feelings.

Anti-whiner Technique

When someone makes you feel guilty, frustrated and helpless through nagging, whining and complaining, you can follow this technique. Usually, people who whine feel overwhelmed, insecure and irritated. Every time you try to help them, they interpret your help as criticism because it shows they are out of control with their own things. On the other hand, if you add a compliment, they will feel endorsed and will quiet down and relax.

To add to the above techniques, you can overcome guilt by developing a perspective. One of the common cognitive distortions that lead to guilt is the misguided notion that you are responsible for the feelings of other people or for events that occur. You have to be crystal clear on the extent to which you can resume responsibility. This is technically referred to as disattribution. Do not carry the entire burden else it will crush you.

7: Cognitive Therapy for Mood Disorders

Depression is considered one of the top public health problems and it is so widespread that it is commonly referred to as the common cold of psychiatric disturbances. Depression kills and this is why studies conducted among adolescents and children indicate shocking increase in suicide rates. The escalating death rates defy the billions of tranquilizers and antidepressant drugs rolled out in the past several decades to help bring the condition under control.

Despite the seemingly gloomy picture, the good news is that depression can be overcome through simple mood elevation methods. A group of psychologists and psychiatrists from the University Of Pennsylvania School Of Medicine developed and tested a new approach to depression and emotional disorders.

Through a series of studies, the practitioners confirmed that the techniques they have developed were effective in reducing the symptoms associated with depression more rapidly compared to drug therapy and conventional psychotherapy. This new approach was named cognitive therapy.

Cognitive therapy is a mood modification technology you can learn on your own. It helps in the elimination of depression symptoms and gives you an opportunity to experience personal growth as a way of helping you cope effectively with depression in the future.

In a nutshell, cognitive therapy provides rapid symptomatic improvement where you experience relief from your symptoms. In addition, it gives you a clear understanding of your mood and the causes behind your powerful emotions as well as self-control where you learn how to apply effective coping strategies that will help you to feel better every time you are upset.

The coping and problem solving strategies that you learn from cognitive therapy cover every crisis there is in modern life. Some of these include divorce, failure, death, as well as problems that have no obvious external cause such as frustration, low self-confidence, apathy and guilt.

Cognitive therapy is among the first forms of psychotherapy that have been subjected to rigorous scientific scrutiny and shown to be effective. It has a professional evaluation and validation at the highest possible academic levels.

Principles of Cognitive Therapy

Unlike traditional psychotherapy, cognitive therapy is neither anti-intuitive nor occult but rather a practical and common sense-based practice that you can practice it on your own. Below are the principles of cognitive therapy.

Your Cognitions Create Your Moods

Cognition refers to your mental attitudes, perception and beliefs. It is the way you interpret things; what you say about yourself or someone else. Even the way you feel now is a result of the thoughts you are thinking at this very moment.

For instance, as you read this book, you may be thinking that cognitive therapy is too good to be true and can never work for you. If you allow your thoughts to run along these lines, you will feel discouraged and skeptical. Remember there is no third party that has induced those feelings but rather a product of your own thoughts.

On the contrary, you may have felt a sudden excitement and uplifting mood because you thought the content of this book may finally help you. Your emotional reaction is dictated not by the text you are reading but the way you are thinking. The moment you have a thought and belief in something, you will immediately experience an emotional response. Your thoughts create the emotion.

Thoughts Dominated by Negativity cause Depression

When you are depressed, your mind shifts to a negative perception. A look into your past only brings forth all the bad things that have ever happened to you. When you look into the future, the only thing you can see is emptiness and unending problems. This bleak vision brings about a sense of hopelessness. In as much as it is absolutely illogical, it seems so real to the point of convincing you that your inadequacy will go on forever.

Negative Thoughts Always Contain Gross Distortions

Negative thoughts appear valid on the surface but at the foundation, they are plain wrong. They cause twisted thinking which brings about suffering. The depression you may be going through is more of a mental slippage than an accurate perception of reality.

Patients treated with cognitive therapy improve much more rapidly than those treated with drugs. Within the first two weeks of continuous and effective cognitive therapy, most patients show a pronounced reduction in negative and suicidal thoughts.

The secret of this success is that unlike drugs, cognitive therapy enables individuals to understand what it is that troubles them and what they can do to cope with it.

The average cognitively treated sufferer experienced a significance elimination of symptoms at the end of the treatment while many of them reported an improvement in their moods. Mood training, which is part of the therapy, brings about confidence and a sense of self-esteem. No matter how depressed, pessimistic or miserable you feel; a persistent and consistent application of cognitive therapy methods will help you recover.

There is no guarantee that after going through the cognitive methods to eliminate depression you will never again have upsets and mood swings. As a matter of fact, getting upset from time to time is part of being human. The assurance, however, is as long as you reapply the cognitive techniques; you will manage to bring the condition under control as you master your moods.

There is a clear difference between, feeling better, which is a spontaneous event and getting better which comes from a systematic application and reapplication of method that will lift your mood even in the most difficult circumstances.

There is a crucial development in modern psychology and psychiatry where the focus is on understanding human emotions. This new approach has drawn in large numbers of mental health professionals interested in providing a solution to the hopelessness and feelings of unworthiness exuded by those going through depression.

8: Choosing to Live – The Ultimate Victory

According to research, about one third of individuals suffering from mild cases of depression and approximately three quarters of people who are severally depressed have suicidal thoughts. There is no age group or professional class that is exempt from suicide. Even celebrities and other famous people have been reported to have committed suicide for various reasons, amongst them depression.

Despite the depressive nature of these statistics, there is a silver lining. Suicide is completely unnecessary and through cognitive techniques, you can overcome and eliminate all your suicidal impulses. Depressed individuals frequently think of suicide because a pessimistic and pervasive vision dominates their thought. To them, life seems nothing but a hellish nightmare. When they look into the past, they remember only the moments of suffering and depression.

When you are depressed, memories of the past are distorted and you cannot seem to conjure up any memories of satisfaction and joy. This will make you erroneously conclude that they do not exist. The critical decision to commit suicide comes from an illogical conviction that your mood cannot improve. Just as most depressed patients do, they support their pessimistic predictions with a huge collection of data which seems to be overwhelmingly convincing to them.

Research indicates that the unrealistic sense of hopelessness is one of the most significant factors in the development of suicidal wishes. Because of your twisted thinking, you create an illusion that you are in a trap from where there seems to be no escape. Your suffering seems unbearable and you conclude that your problems are insoluble.

It is important for you to isolate the suicidal impulses that are most threatening. Do not be afraid to discuss them with a counselor as some people are fearful of disapproval or judgment. Discussing your thoughts with a professional therapist will give you relief and a much better chance of eliminating them.

Your life is similar to a chain with a series of interconnected links. Throughout the previous chapters, we have been working towards identifying all those links and now it is time to bring together everything you have gathered so that it can add meaning to your life.

All the fears and distorted thought processes were chains that controlled you and held you back from experiencing your freedom. Your self-concept, whether authentic or fictional, is a product of a chain link from your past into the present and into the future. This continuity may either be positive or negative and it affects who you are at present.

The ability to change the momentum by breaking your chain and starting a new one is completely dependent on you. Once you identify the links from your past that control your present experiences, it would be much easier to know where to focus your energy.

If your history predicts your future and you want a new future then you should start by creating a new history. Your challenge is to break from the old thinking and come in with a new mindset. Ensuring that the old thinking is completely gone is very important because it takes off your blinders and exposes exactly the parts of your past thinking that were tied to your present thought pattern.

Your external experiences in life as well as your internal reactions have carved out a self-concept that has defined you throughout your life. You have constantly pounded on yourself with internal perceptions and self-talk and in turn you have been pounded on and shaped by the behaviors and messages of those you have interacted with in life.

In view of all that, it is now time to create an opportunity to become the blacksmith of your own life. It is time you stopped being passively shaped by internal and external forces in your life and consciously starting to challenge and direct the course of your own life. This will move your self-concept and behavior from the world-defined end which is fictional towards the self-defined and authentic end which is factual.

You have to deliberately start moving towards a new direction and get rid of your old way of thinking that was grounded in your outdated and irrelevant history. It is possible for you to create a momentum that will give you the opportunity to do what you truly value.

In order to redefine your thought process and revolutionize your self-concept, you must commit to be totally honest to evaluate yourself constantly and use all the information and insight you learn to correct and shape your behavior. You must be action-oriented and accountable to effectively deal with your situation and make critical changes.

Working on Your Self-Awareness

Thinking differently becomes almost impossible if we do not pay sufficient attention to the way we think currently. Many people are afraid of exploring and acknowledging their own emotions and thoughts and choose instead to focus on external events and circumstances such as career goals and the needs of others. Focusing on self-awareness can help you reconnect with your dreams, desires and needs.

Increased self-awareness can help you facilitate major life changes. Identifying your emotions and moods will give you the opportunity to adjust them and to reflect your authentic self.

Getting Out Of Your Comfort Zone

Doing the same activities in the same manner day after day will shrink your understanding of your thought process and convert you into an automatic being. Each one of us has a natural tendency to stick to a familiar life and thought process to avoid situations that make us uncomfortable. If we are to grow in our thinking and control our lives, we have to dare the impossible irrespective of how difficult and sticky they are.

Pushing yourself to embrace new thinking dimensions will get you out of your rut and change how you feel about situations and circumstances. Since everything else around remains constant, the only person who can change everything around yourself is you.

Your feelings are a sum total of all your thought processes whether negative or positive. By setting your sails and launching into the deep, you will discover how exhilarating and satisfying your new life is.

Conclusion

Taking control of your mind is the sure way of living a more positive and happy life. Each second, thousands of thoughts infiltrate your mind some which may be conscious and self-imposed while others purely subconscious. The sad reality is that most of these thoughts are distorted and filled with negativity whether you are aware of it or not. Irrespective of your age, ethnicity, level of happiness and gender, negative thinking affects all of us at different times in our lives.

The main problem is that negative thoughts are often hard to diagnose and habitually create an overwhelming effect in our minds. Every one of us has had a bad day where everything seems to be going wrong. The sequence of bad occurrences in our lives initiates a sequence of thought patterns that slowly get out of hand and snowball into something bigger.

A single negative feeling has the capacity to lead to several others making it difficult to get back into action. When you allow negative thoughts to control your mind, they will overcome and consume you within a short time.

Thoughts are rooted deep inside our minds and determine what the rest of the body system does.

While you may not be able to take control of every thought process that comes into your mind, you have the ability to choose and act on the ones you think on a conscious level. Conscious thoughts are usually a reaction to some action. Negative actions generate negative thoughts that in turn allow negativity and pessimism to penetrate our minds.

Instead of blaming yourself and reacting in a negative way, the best approach is to acknowledge the cause of the problem and handle it in a more positive manner. Never allow negative thinking to take control of your life because it will grow and develop into a bad habit that would be difficult to root out.

To avert negative thinking, you need to know that the negative obstacles that you encounter in life are merely temporary barriers and not permanent roadblocks. This way, you will find it easier to let go and concentrate on the positive attributes.

Take every opportunity as a moment of learning something new and a chance to replace negative thoughts with positive ones. Talk back to self-created criticisms and look at life with optimistic lenses. Every positive thought that you experience will help you in overpowering the negative ones. This will change how you feel and your life as a whole.

www.ingramcontent.com/pod-product-compliance
Lightning Source LLC
LaVergne TN
LVHW050032030125
800366LV00027B/1135